HAZEL MIST
Hypnotist

by Kristin Pierce

Illustrated by Abbey Bryant

Inner Compass
Books

This story begins with a young Hazel Mist,
Who sat down to watch a famous hypnotist.
Interest consumed her. She was glued to the show.
She watched till the end 'cause she just had to know.

Quite perplexed, Hazel asked,
"Dad, how does that work?"
"It's beyond me, darling,"
Dad said with a smirk.

Her jaw hit the floor; eyes peeled wide with wonder.

Inspiration rolled right through her like thunder.

Hazel's mind was soaring while cleaning the perch,
So she borrowed dad's phone for an internet search.

"How to learn hypnosis" is what she typed in;
While bright-eyed with passion—lit up with a grin.

Straight to the library, she went to devour
Every book she could find, for hour after hour.

She absorbed, took notes, practiced, and then pondered.
From dawn right till dusk—that summer she conquered.

Hazel practiced, rehearsed, and performed on her friends,
While stretching her mind to unthinkable ends.

Then she knew it was time
to get up on a stage
To put herself out there
and learn to engage.

So, she built her routine—
tried, tested, and true.
And then it was time
for her public debut.

Butterflies in her tummy;
    churning like a storm.
Her cheeks turned bright red.
    She felt clammy and warm.

Yes, Hazel was nervous,
    felt scared half to death.
So she settled her nerves
    and took a deep breath.

Then she mustered the courage
    to step out on stage.
Calmly talked herself through,
    step-by-step, like a sage:

"First, welcome your crowd—
    make them feel just like friends.
To get them to trust you,
    this time you must spend."

"Give them distractions;
    now, show them the facts
To lower their guards and
    to help them relax.

Next, give fun suggestions
    to get them involved;
To loosen them up and
    let fear be resolved.

The crowd's all warmed up.
    Now, it's time to begin.
Stay cool and stay steady—
    envision the win."

"Now, bark! Wag your tail; you're a cute little dog.

You're a lumberjack team that's sawing a log."

TIMBER!

"Relax on the beach at your favourite spot.

You're a pro surfer. Show us what you've got."

Before each performance, she gave a pep talk
To herself in the mirror, then on stage she'd walk.

"Just trust yourself, Hazel, and follow your flow.
Take one more deep breath, now get on with the show."

"Surprise! You're a flash mob—
Perform your routine.

Go! Start your chef challenge,
make cheesy poutine.

You can fly like a bird—
Show us how you soar.

You're zen'd out at yoga—
melt stress to the floor."

With each show completed, Miss Hazel had found
The lessons and learnings were deeply profound.
Under hypnosis, Hazel soon did notice
Truth would rise up from the depths like a lotus.

It was wildly intriguing; wide-eyed through the night,
Her eager excitement had turned on a light.
It sparked deeper interest (she hadn't expected),
So she followed her compass to where it directed.

Diving into the theory beneath all the frills,
Hazel learned all she could to hone her new skills.
She connected the dots and researched the mind,
Then was just blown away with what she did find . . .

"Thinking builds limits
    where there's actually none!
When we believe blocks,
    we stop dreams and lose fun."

This huge realization
    smacked her in the chest;
First, it melted her fear,
    then rerouted her quest.

Instead of just laughter, Hazel saw potential . . .

"To educate minds
could be so influential."

Her crowd sure did grow—yes, they wanted a show
And Hazel would dazzle each row upon row.

Her show, too, had grown a unique, special feature:
Each performance led her crowd deeper and deeper.

"You're a curling team. Hurry hard! Sweep that rock!

Now one-at-a-time, cannonball off the dock."

"Go sing your heart out. Share your deepest desires.

Give a world-class speech that moves hearts and inspires."

"Here's the greatest magician—Miss, let's see some fun.

You're the fastest cube champion. Show us how it's done."

"Now, please would you show us your best goat parkour."

The show's grand finale sparked laughter galore.

"Weren't they entertaining?! Yes—laughter is healing!
But there's more underneath that's deeply revealing.

Hypnosis bypasses the great thinking mind,
And makes space for healing that's truly aligned."

"Did you notice, you sir,
  forgot your knee pain?

Your stress disappeared—
  isn't that just insane?

You came out of your shell!
  Can you imagine?!
And filled this whole room
  with such palpable passion."

"You spoke from your soul—
it was moving and bold.

Your inner magic
was a sight to behold.

You solved this cube in
well under a minute."

"If you think you CAN'T or believe that you CAN,
Your mind is determined to stick to your plan.
But all of these 'blocks' you believe to be true
Are not in your way—they don't have to stop you.

So, pull back the curtain and then shine a light
On the 'limits' and 'blocks' that just don't feel right."

WORRY

GUILT

ANG

LF-
EEM

NER

INNER
CRITIC

RAID

E

SHY

BLAME

DOUBT

TE

ARED

WEAKNESS

FEAR

JUDGMENT

OBSTA

TOO
OLD

EXCUSES

LIMITS

LABELS

SCARED

LACK

CRITICS

FAILURE

T
YO

"And if that's all it takes to melt fear and break walls,
Were you ever restricted? A little? At all?

So question your limits, then shoot for the stars.
'Cause the big dreams we dream are meant to be ours."

"Master your mindset, and the hard work is done.
When you follow your heart, you have already won."

"Pursue all your passions, and give yourself room
To grow and explore and to blossom and bloom.
'Cause all of your 'limits' can rip at the seams
When you harness your courage and go for your dreams."

"The world needs what you've got—
    it's your time to soar.
So, spread out your wings.
    You are destined for more."

"It all lives within you.
Folks, you saw it here.
You're full of potential.
Go live without fear."

Reflection Questions

"Reading without reflecting is like eating without digesting."
-Edmund Burke

Hazel Mist was awe-struck when she watched a famous hypnotist on TV.
She was consumed with curiosity and just had to know more.
Have you had inspiration strike you in a similar way?
What were you intrigued by?

Hazel did not have anyone to teach her about hypnotism,
so she took matters into her own hands and went to the library.
Is there a topic or skill that you would like to learn more about?
How could you do your own research?
Where could you go? Who could you ask for help?

While researching, Hazel practiced the techniques that she was
reading about to help deepen her understanding. What are some
ways that you could put into practice what you are learning?

What might have happened to Hazel if she was too scared to
get up on stage to follow her dreams? What steps did she
take to calm herself down and give herself courage?

Have you ever felt nervous or scared to do something new?
What did you do to help calm your nerves?

Hazel shared a new way for her audience to open their minds, shift their
perspectives, and spark self-reflection. In reading Hazel Mist, Hypnotist,
which questions came to mind for you? How did your perspective shift?

Hazel discovered that our limits only have power because we believe them.
What limits have you been believing about yourself that just aren't true?

Has there ever been a time when you quit something
because you didn't think you could do it?
Next time, what could you do to shift your perspective and give it a try?

"The big dreams we dream are meant to be ours."
What wild dreams would you go after, if you knew that anything was possible?

For FREE mind-stretching activities for the young minds in your life,
visit our website at www.InnerCompassBooks.com/learning-resource

About the Author

Photo by Nancy Newby Photography

Just like Hazel Mist, Kristin Pierce followed her curiosity, which led her on an unexpected learning adventure deep into the workings of the mind. Captivated by how limiting beliefs compress the wild possibilities available to us at any given moment, she began to witness the transformation that is possible when we question our self-talk, perceived limits, and fears that box us in.

Kristin Pierce is an award-winning author, the founder of Inner Compass Books, and a self-awareness educator. It is her mission to create mindfully-crafted children's books that encourage readers to question their limits, trust their inner knowing, and dream bigger than belief.

Kristin lives in Saskatchewan, Canada with her husband, two children, and their dog.

Hazel Mist, Hypnotist is her fifth children's book.

Other Titles from Inner Compass Books:

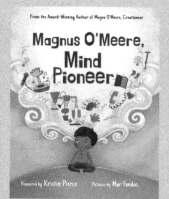
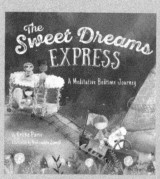

For FREE learning resources, mad libs, and more, visit **www.InnerCompassBooks.com** and follow Inner Compass Books on Facebook and Instagram @InnerCompassBooks.

Dedication:

To everyone who ever thought, "I can't." I promise you it's just not true.
And to all of my mind mentors along the way, thank you for sharing your wisdom.

Note from the Author:

Hazel Mist, Hypnotist was mindfully crafted to spark curiosity, kick-start self-reflection, and open a door in the mind of the reader. I believe that passion is the rocket fuel that blasts through mental barriers, gives courage to move through fear, and ignites a fire within to pursue one's vision. It is my hope that Hazel Mist will spark that insight within you.

Acknowledgements:

Thank you to my readers, my family, and my team for supporting me in the creation of Inner Compass Books.
To all of my mental mentors along the way, thank you for sharing your wisdom and for opening my mind.
Abbey, thank you for sharing your artistic talent to bring little Miss Hazel to life.
Lacy, thank you for your editing expertise, support, and wonderful guidance along the way.
To my kids, thank you for being my creative sidekicks, my sounding boards, and the reason I write.
Thank you to my husband for his unwavering patience and support, and for enduring my never-ending (and sometimes one-sided) conversations that come with any project I set out to create.

Hazel Mist, Hypnotist
Copyright © 2020 by Kristin Pierce

Written by: Kristin Pierce
Illustrated by: Abbey Bryant
Edited by: Lacy Lieffers of One Leaf Editing
Art direction, book layout, and cover design by: Kristin Pierce

ISBN
978-1-99908-812-5 (Hardcover)
978-1-99908-813-2 (Paperback)
Find us on Facebook and Instagram @ InnerCompassBooks, and stay tuned for more book magic coming your way.

Inner Compass Books.com